Those Mean, Nasty, Dirty, Downright Disgusting but... INVISIBLE Germs

Written by Judith Rice
Illustrated by Reed Merrill

Redleaf Press
St. Paul, Minnesota

© 1989 Judith Rice

© 1989 Cover Design and Drawings: Reed Merrill

© 1989 Photography: David Mastbaum

ISBN: 0-934140-46-4

Library of Congress Number: 89-34409

Published by   Redleaf Press
                      a division of Resources for Child Caring
                      450 North Syndicate Suite 5
                      St. Paul, Minnesota 55104

Distributed by   Gryphon House

Library of Congress Cataloging-in-Publication Data

Rice, Judith
     Those mean nasty dirty downright disgusting but— invisible
germs / written by Judith Rice ; illustrated by Reed Merrill.
           p.   cm.
     Summary: A little girl, who accumulates germs on her hands
during her busy day, defeats them by washing her hands before meals.
       1. Children— Health and hygiene— Juvenile literature.
2. Bacteria— Juvenile literature. 3. Viruses— Juvenile literature.
[1. Bacteria. 2. Viruses. 3. Health.] I. Merrill, Reed, ill. II. Title.
RA777.R53 1989   589.9— dc20   89-34409
ISBN: 0-934140-46-4

Printed in Hong Kong by South China Printing Co.

This book is dedicated to

Reed, Rosemary, Emily and Benjamin Merrill
Sylvester and Theresa Eller
William and Lucille Rice
My family
Friends
The Early Childhood Family Education Program

Special thanks to Beth Marie Schanzenbach, who
portrays her beautiful spirited self in this book.

We are fortunate to live in a land which is free of many of the serious infectious diseases of the past, such as small pox, typhoid fever, and cholera. The control of these diseases was achieved through public health measures which included vaccines and the prevention of spread of infection. Important in the latter was the purification of water and food and the safe disposal of human wastes. These successes were not achieved easily, and our generation owes much to those who did this work.

It has proved even more difficult to control infections which are spread by personal contact. In these infections, good personal hygiene plays an important role in control. This book introduces the subject of personal hygiene in a way which is scientifically sound and relevant to the abilities and motivational capacity of the small child.

Jack M. Gwaltney, Jr., M.D.
Professor of Internal Medicine
Head, Division of Epidemiology and Virology
University of Virginia School of Medicine

This is Beth. She is five years old.
One day when she was at school...

painting the most beautiful rainbow, a mean, nasty, dirty, downright disgusting, but invisible germ got on her hand. The kind that can give you an earache. And if you could see it,

maybe it would look like...

this!

The next germ came along while Beth was building a space station with wooden blocks.

It was a mean, nasty, dirty, downright disgusting, but invisible germ. The kind that can give you a headache. And if you could see it,

maybe it would look like...

this!

While Beth was reading the most interesting story, a mean, nasty, dirty, downright disgusting but invisible germ got on her hand. The kind that can give you a sore throat. And if you could see it,

maybe it would look like...

this!

Next, Beth was pretending to be all grown up, when a mean, nasty, dirty, downright disgusting but invisible germ got on her hand. The kind that can give you a temperature. And if you could see it,

maybe it would look like...

this!

Then last, but not least, the **worst, most horrible, mean, nasty, dirty, downright disgusting but invisible** germ of all got on her hand while she was driving her truck to Alaska. It's the kind that makes you throw up! And if you could see it,

it might look like...

this!

Now Beth's hands were covered with
mean, nasty, dirty, downright
disgusting but invisible germs.

Thank goodness Beth knows what
everybody needs to know—
how to get RID of germs.

Before lunch, Beth washed her hands with lots of soap and water.

She couldn't hear them, but while she rubbed and scrubbed, rinsed and rubbed and scrubbed...

"Yikes!" screamed the germ that can give you an earache as it went swirling, whirling down the drain.

"Foiled again!" shouted the germ that can give you a headache as it went swirling, whirling down the drain.

"Whoa...haa...ah!" cried out the germ that gives you a sore throat as it went swirling, whirling down the drain.

"Oh no!" steamed the germ that gives you a fever as it went swirling, whirling down the drain.

Now, do you think that was the end of all those horrible germs???

Oh, no...

There was one germ left. The meanest, nastiest, downright disgustingest, but most invisiblest germ of all. The one that makes you throw up!

It was hiding out in the palm of Beth's hand.

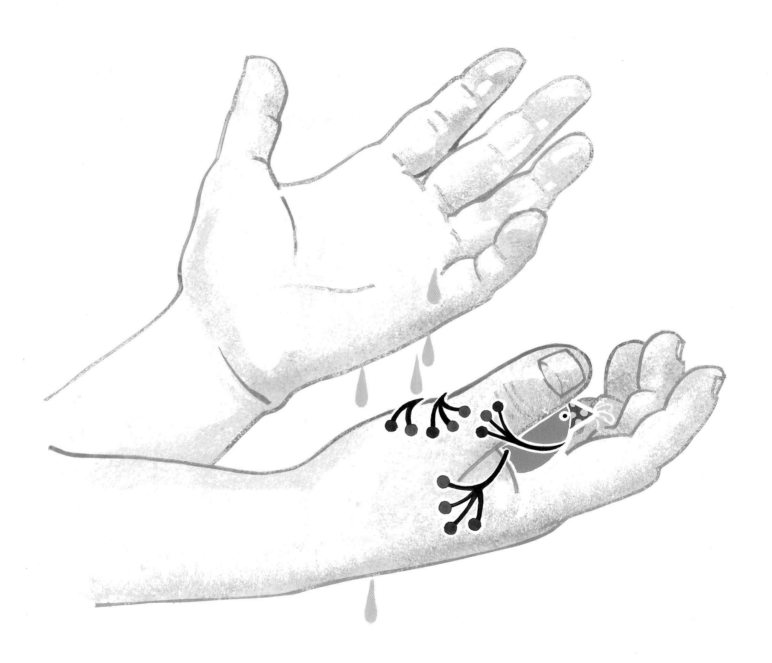

Germs like wet places, and Beth's hands were wet from washing.

Germs like warm places (and our bodies are always warm).

But being the wonderfully intelligent child that Beth is, she knew all about what germs like.

So she carefully dried her hands.

She couldn't hear it, but the germ that makes you throw up said, **"I'll be back!"** as Beth threw it away into the waste paper basket.

Beth picked up her peanut butter and banana sandwich with her clean, germ-free hands, took a bite, and said, "Simply delicious!"

And even though she knew that all those mean nasty dirty downright disgusting but invisible germs would be back, Beth felt safe and happy because she knows what everyone needs to know—

handwashing gets RID of germs.

Other Redleaf Press Publications

Basic Guide to Family Day Care Record Keeping — Clear instructions on keeping necessary family day care business records.

Calendar-Keeper — Activities, family day care record keeping, recipes and more. Updated annually. Most popular publication in the field.

Child Care Resource & Referral Counselors & Trainers Manual — Both a ready reference for the busy phone counselor and a training guide for resource and referral agencies.

The Dynamic Infant — Combines an overview of child development with innovative movement and sensory experiences for infants and toddlers.

Family Day Care Tax Workbook — Updated every year, latest step-by-step information on forms, depreciation, etc.

The Kids Encyclopedia of Things to Make and Do — Nearly 2,000 art and craft projects for children aged 4-10.

Open the Door, Let's Explore — Full of fun, inexpensive neighborhood walks and field trips designed to help young children.

Practical Solutions to Practically Every Problem : The Early Childhood Teacher's Manual — Over 300 proven developmentally appropriate solutions for all kinds of classroom problems.

Roots & Wings: Affirming Culture in Early Childhood Programs — A new approach to multicultural education that helps shape positive attitudes toward cultural differences.

Sharing in the Caring — Packets with family day care parent brochure, contracts and hints.

Staff Orientation in Early Childhood Programs — Complete manual for orienting new staff on all program areas.

Survival Kit for Early Childhood Directors — Solutions, implementation steps and results to handling difficulties with children, staff, parents.

Teachables From Trashables — Step-by-step guide to making over 50 fun toys from recycled household junk.

Teachables II — Similar to above; with another 75-plus toys.

Trusting Toddlers: Planning for One to Three Year Olds in Child Care Centers — Expert panel explains how to set up toddler programs that really work.